The SST Therapist's Pocket Companion

The SST Therapist's Pocket Companion

Windy Dryden

Rationality Publications

Rationality Publications
136 Montagu Mansions, London W1U 6LQ

www.rationalitypublications.com
info@rationalitypublications.com

First edition published by Rationality Publications
Copyright (c) 2022 Windy Dryden

The right of Windy Dryden to be identified as the
author of this work has been asserted in accordance
with sections 77 and 78 of the Copyright Designs and
Patents Act 1988.

A catalogue record of this book is
available from the British Library.

First edition 2022

ISBN: 978-1-914938-02-3

Introduction

I have compiled the material in this book and have presented it in this format to remind busy trained and developing single-session therapists of what is generally regarded as important principles concerning the nature and practice of SST. These principles are presented briefly for handy reference.

As such, let me discourage you from reading this book in one sitting. If you do, you will get severe clinical indigestion. For these 150 principles are meant to be considered one at a time, savoured even, as a way of prompting self-reflection about your SST thinking and practice. Thus, if you discover an area of SST where you struggle, my hope is that you may find something in this book that might help you deal productively with your struggle in an easily remembered form. As such, the book is designed to be kept in your pocket so that you can consult it when you need a timely reminder of a point of good SST practice.

This is why I have called the book *The SST Therapist's Pocket Companion.*

Please note that while this book can be used by all SST therapists, I have written it largely for those working with adult individuals. It is my hope that experienced SST therapists who work with families, couples and children and adolescents might write a similar pocket companion for use with these populations.

Windy Dryden
London, Eastbourne
July 2021

❏ Give careful thought to how you portray SST on your website or that of the agency where you work. The website description may help shape your clients' expectations and save valuable time later.

❑ In SST, you are trying to integrate two seemingly different ideas: helping the client leave the session with what they have come for and providing them with additional help, if needed.

❏ Remember that SST is not one session and one session only ... unless you and your client have agreed that it should be.

❏ While single-session therapy can be by default or by design, its therapeutic potency is enhanced in the latter case.

❏ Remember from your own personal
experience that a brief encounter
can be therapeutic.

❑ Remember that effective therapy
can take place in the time allocated
to it.

❏ Remember that change may have begun to happen from the point the person decided to seek help.

❏ Remember that the modal number of sessions clients have internationally across agencies is '1', followed by '2', followed by '3', etc.

❏ Remember that you won't be able to predict with accuracy whether a client will attend for one session or more.

❑ Please do not automatically think that a client who decides not to return for a second session has 'dropped out' of therapy.

❏ There is a good chance that when a client decides not to come back for a second session that they were satisfied with what they got from the first.

❏ Some people will come for a number of single therapy sessions each at the time of their choosing.

❑ Some help now is better than the best help later, unless the client decides otherwise.

❏ In SST, less is often more and more
is often less.

❏ SST is a blend of what the client brings to the session and what you, as a therapist, bring to the session.

❏ SST is pluralistic in nature. As such you will need to work with both/and rather than either/or. Thus, in a single session at different times, for example, you may take *both* a neutral listening stance *and* a focused questioning stance.

❏ Human beings have the capability to help themselves quickly under specific circumstances. These are:

➤ knowing how to change and acting on that knowledge
➤ having a committed reason to change and
➤ being prepared to accept the costs of change.

❏ SST is open to all clients who want it.

❏ It is paradoxical but true that clients are often happier with a single session when they know that further help is available.

❏ At the person's very first contact with an SST service, be responsive, attentive and accessible. Outline SST and explain the process. This will help the person to make an informed decision concerning SST.

❏ If possible, help the client to prepare for the session by questionnaire or by phone.

❏ Encourage the client to understand that preparing for the session will help them to get the most from it.

❑ Remember that the best way to discover if a client can benefit from a single session is to give them a single session and see if they benefit from it.

☐ Help your client at the point of their need rather than at the point of appointment availability.

☐ Much can be achieved if the client is ready to change and you can capitalise on that readiness.

❏ While real therapeutic change may happen slowly and gradually it can also happen quickly and suddenly.

❑ SST is not a specific approach to therapy. It is a way of working with clients informed by the single-session mindset and by a variety of different therapeutic approaches.

❏ Different ways of working therapeutically with clients require different therapeutic mindsets. Make sure you bring a single-session mindset to single-session therapy.

❏ It is useful to get into the 'single-session mindset' before you begin the session.

❏ If you need a reminder about the purpose and power of a single session, review the following statement by Slive, McElheran & Lawson (2008: 6) who, writing about walk-in SST say that it:

'Enables clients to meet with a mental health professional at their moment of choosing. There is no red tape, no triage, no intake process, no wait list, and no wait. There is no formal assessment, no formal diagnostic process, just one hour of therapy focused on clients' stated wants....Also, with walk-in therapy there are no missed appointments or cancellations, thereby increasing efficiency'

❏ If you and your client both expect
change from SST, it is much more
likely to happen than if both of
you do not expect it. So, expect
your client to change, they just
might do so.

❏ Remember that you communicate your expectations covertly as well as overtly to the client concerning how much change you think that they are likely to make. So make your covert expectations consistent with your overt expectations on this point.

❑ Approach the session as if it could be the last.

❏ View the session as a whole, complete in itself.

❏ Remember that 'this may be it'.
This may be the only opportunity
that you have to help the client.
Will you capture it or let it slip?

❏ Use the power of 'now'. Because now is all you have.

❑ At the outset, ensure that the client understands SST and has provided their informed consent before proceeding.

❏ Remember no matter how much knowledge and skill you bring to the session, the power is in the client.

❏ Unless your client has suggested that you adopt a passive listening stance, you need to be active in the session yourself. As you do so, remember that you also need to encourage your client to be an active participant in the session.

❏   There are many ways to begin a
     session. Use one that works best for
     you, but have others in reserve.

❏ If you favour beginning the session by asking the client about their understanding of the purpose of SST, ask:

'From your perspective, what is the purpose of our conversation today?'

❏ If you favour beginning the session by asking the client about their problem, concern or issue, ask:

'What problem, concern or issue would you like to discuss with me?'

or

'What problem, concern or issue would you like me to help you with?'

❑ If you favour beginning the session by asking the client about their goal, ask:

'What would you like to achieve by talking with me today?'

or

'What would you like to take away from our conversation that would make it worthwhile that you came today?'

❑ If you favour beginning the session by asking the client about what help they are seeking, ask:

'How can I be most helpful to you today?'

or

'What help would you like from me today?'

❏ If the client says that they want to learn some tools to deal with their problem, bear in mind that the concept of 'tools' is broad enough to cover a wealth of ways that you can help the person deal with their problem.

❑ If the client says that they want to learn a technique to deal with their problem, accept this, but tell them that you first need to understand the problem and what they want to achieve from discussing it with you. Then, armed with this information you can both select the most appropriate technique.

❏ If you favour beginning the session by issuing an open invitation for the client to begin in whichever way they choose, you might say something like:

'We have 50 minutes together and I will be glad to hear whatever you wish to tell me.'

❑ If necessary, explain what you can do and what you cannot do in SST. Be transparent.

❏ If the agency in which you work mandates you to carry out certain activities, begin the session after you have carried out these activities. However, explain this to the client before you begin and get their agreement.

❏ In single-session therapy help the person who happens to have a particular diagnosis with what they want to take away from the session. Do not be blinded by the diagnosis.

❏ Show the client that you are keen to help them as quickly as possible.

❑ Convey to the client that you are
willing to work hard to help them
deal with their issue and invite them
to join you by doing the same.

❑ Plan the session according to the time available. If you only have 20 minutes with a client, use that time effectively.

❏ Begin therapy immediately.

❏ An effective working alliance can be established quickly in SST.

❏ Aim for relational promptness
rather than for relational depth.

❏ If you think that the client is at risk,
your priority is to safeguard them.
Doing so is a valid use of the single
session.

❏ At the beginning of the session, ask the client what they have done between completing the pre-session questionnaire and the session that may have brought about change. Then, capitalise on that change.

❏ Remember that the client determines the direction of the session, not you.

❏ Allow your client to determine how much help they need at any particular time.

❏ There is a lot of information you don't need to know about your client. Only ask them for information that will help you help them.

❏ Instead of taking a case history, ask the client to tell you what *they* think is essential for you to know in order for you to help them in the session.

❑   Discover which helping stance your
    client wants you to take. Do they
    want you to help them:

    ➼ explore an issue
    ➼ understand an issue better
    ➼ express their feelings about an
      issue
    ➼ make a decision about an issue or
    ➼ solve an emotional problem?

❏ If a client wants to understand an issue better or to express their feelings about an issue, ask them what they hope that doing these things will lead to. Then work with their reply as their goal.

❏ Adopt your client's chosen helping stance unless you think that there is a good reason not to do so. If so, be clear about your reasoning with the client.

❑ Complex problems do not always require complex solutions.

❏ Therapists who work in single-session walk-in services have shown us that clients who have severe and complex problems can benefit from single-session therapy. For such clients, it is an agreed focus on one issue for which they can take away a solution and implement that is empowering for them.

❏ If your client says 'I don't know', suggest some options to stimulate their thinking.

❏ If the client wants focused help, encourage them to create a focus for the session.

❑ Once you have agreed a focus with the client encourage them to stay with that focus.

❑ Change the focus if the client realises that another issue has greater priority for them.

❏ Give the client a rationale for the possibility that you may interrupt them so that you can both maintain the agreed focus. Ask the client for permission to interrupt them after they have understood the rationale.

❏ Strive to be clear in all your communications with your client.

❏ Check out if you have been clear by asking your client to share their understanding of what you have said.

❏ Explain what you are doing and why you are doing, but do not do so compulsively.

❏ Offer your client your expertise without assuming the role of expert.

❏ You don't have the time to carry out a full case formulation, but you can be informed by case formulation principles.

❑ There is no single protocol or manual for the effective practice of SST. If someone offers one to you, politely decline.

❏ Encourage the client to focus on a problem that can be solved rather than one that can't be solved.

❑ When discussing an example of the client's nominated problem, use an imminent example if possible. Doing so will help the client to implement the selected solution in the same situation in which you have both done the work.

❏ Communicate your understanding
of the client's nominated problem
from their frame of reference.

❏ Assess the client's nominated problem using both their ideas and concepts from your favoured therapy approach and other relevant approaches.

❏ Help the client deal with the adversity that features in their nominated problem if at all possible.

❏ Get to the heart of the matter if you can.

❏ Draw the client's attention to important points in their narrative to see what they think of these points.

❏ Have the client understand how they have unwittingly maintained their nominated problem.

❑ Target for change your client's subsequent responses to their initial reaction rather than the initial reaction itself.

❏ If you can, identify and work with the key mechanism. This is the factor that explains the existence of the client's problem, and which needs to be changed if the client is going to achieve their problem-related goal.

❏ If relevant, help the client to set a goal concerning their nominated problem.

❏ Help the client to see the connection between their session goal and their problem-related goal.

❏ If relevant, ask the client what they are prepared to sacrifice to achieve their problem-related goal.

❏ Remember that sometimes the client's goal is the problem (e.g. 'I want to eliminate my anxiety').

❑ Helping a client take a few steps forward may help them to travel the rest of the journey without professional assistance.

❏ A client often comes to SST 'stuck'. Help them to get 'unstuck' and move forward.

❏ Discover what the client has done in the past to try to solve the problem. Encourage them to:

→ Utilise what was helpful and
→ Cast aside what was not helpful.

❏ Look for instances where the client
has solved similar problems and
encourage them to consider
applying what they did to solve
these problems to solving their
nominated problem.

❏ Discover the client's strengths and encourage them to utilise those that are relevant to solving their nominated problem.

❏ If the client cannot come up with any strengths, encourage them to think about what a loved one would say their strengths were or ask them to imagine them responding to a question about their strengths at an interview for a job they really want.

❑ Look for exceptions to the client's problem and build on these exceptions.

❏ Look for instances that the client's goal is already happening or has happened in the past. Build on such instances.

❏ Discover and work with the client's values.

❏ Discover and make use of the client's nominated role models.

❏ Ask the client what music inspires
them. Encourage them to make use
of this music after the session to
inspire them to implement the
selected solution.

❏ Ask the client whether they can think of any inspiring poetry or literature to which they can refer when initiating change.

❏ Ask the client what life lessons they have learned. Encourage them to make use of these lessons in the change process.

❏ Discover and encourage the use of any maxims the client finds helpful and that they can apply in the change process. Mine is 'If you don't ask, you don't get. But remember that asking doesn't guarantee getting.'

❑ Encourage the client to advise a
friend facing the same problem and
work with the obstacles to applying
their suggested solution to themself.

❏ Ask the client to reflect on how others have solved the same problem and how they might make use of others' experience on this issue.

❏ Use metaphors, parables and stories
with your client when appropriate.

❏ Consider using self-disclosure to make a point that may help take the client forward. First, ask for permission to do so and afterwards ask what the client has learned from your experience.

❏ When using self-disclosure as an SST therapist, only do so if you have struggled with a similar issue with which the client is struggling and have dealt effectively with it.

❏ Educate your client when they seem to lack information, but not when they don't.

❏ Discover external resources that the client may draw upon to help them with their nominated problem.

❑ Encourage your client to nominate and make use of people in their life who are on their 'team'. Different people on their team can provide different forms of help.

❏ Look for ways of making an impact on your client without forcing the issue.

❏ Identify and respond to any doubts, reservations and objections (DROs) the client may have concerning any aspect of the session.

❏ Encourage the client to summarise periodically what has gone on in the session. Doing so will help to progress the session.

❑ Recognise that change comes in different forms:

- ✦ attitude change
- ✦ inference change
- ✦ behavioural change
- ✦ environmental change or
- ✦ a combination of the above

Your client will decide which type of change is best for them.

❏ A small change for the client may be sufficient. Do not overload them.

❏ Don't try and be brilliant. Be helpful.

❏ Don't rush. You have more time than you think you do.

❏ Give yourself time to think and process when you need to do so.

❑ Give the client time to think and process throughout the session.

❏ Don't cram too much into the session.

❏ Use the client's own words rather than synonyms.

❏ Ask the client to repeat important
   things that they have just said
   (Dryden's 'deaf old man'
   technique).

❏ Use humour judiciously.

❏ In helping the client construct a solution to their nominated problem encourage them to draw upon relevant factors already discussed. These may include:

- their strengths
- relevant external resources
- helpful aspects of previously used attempts to solve the nominated problem
- general helping strategies that they have used in the past with other problems
- constructive alternatives to problem maintaining factors
- their own views on what may be helpful in solving the problem
- your views on what may be helpful in solving the problem

❏ Ensure that any solution the client
selects can be integrated by them
into their life.

❏ Encourage the client to select a solution that they are most likely to implement.

❑ Encourage the client to rehearse the
solution in the session.

❑ Help the client to develop a plan to implement the solution.

❑ Encourage the client to identify and problem-solve any obstacles to implementing the action plan.

❑ If possible, help the client to generalise their learning.

❏ Monte Bobele (2021) has said that in general SST practitioners want their clients to end the session with:

+ a sense that they have been heard
+ increased hope and decreased stress
+ increased awareness of strengths and resources and how to make use of them
+ perhaps a new way to think about a problem
+ perhaps a 'next step' for addressing a problem
+ a positive experience of psychotherapy

❏ Towards the end of the session, ask the client to provide a final summary.

❏ Encourage the client to take away something meaningful from the session.

❏ Help the client to think of a pithy saying to express what they have learned from the session.

❑ Before ending the session, commend the client for their strengths and resources and for their active work in the session.

❏ If the client's take-away is different from the solution, find something that links the two.

❏ Be mindful about time but do not be ruled by time limits in SST. End 'early' if you and the client have finished 'early'.

❑ When ending the session, engender hope in the client that they will be able to take away something meaningful from the session which they can apply in their life.

❏ Before ending the session, encourage the client to tell you anything about the issue that they might regret not telling you or to ask you anything about the issue that they might regret not asking you.

❏ At the end of the session, revisit the issue of further help for the client.

❑ If the client says that they need no further help at the end of the session, proceed to the follow-up stage.

❏ If the client says that they are not sure if they want further help at the end of the session, encourage them to go away and reflect on and digest what they learned in the session, put what they learned into practice and let time pass before making a decision about further help.

❑ If the client says that they need further help at the end of the session, discuss with them what additional help they need and what can be offered by you or by the agency where you work.

❏ Seek client feedback. It will help you develop as an SST therapist.

❑ Set a follow-up date at a time ideally chosen by the client unless your agency has a set policy on this issue.

❑ Consider engaging in some of the following activities to further your development as an SST therapist:

- Get training in SST if you have not already done so
- Get regular supervision of your work where you discuss that work and play audio-recordings of your sessions to your supervisor
- Engage in relevant CPD activities
- Read the SST literature
- Seek SST for yourself for any relevant issues that you may need help with

References

Bobele, M. (2021). *Introducing Single-Session / Walk-In Therapy: An Emergent Form of Service Delivery*. Continuing Education Program. Washington, DC: American Psychological Association.

Slive, A., McElheran, N., & Lawson, A. (2008). How brief does it get? Walk-in single session therapy. *Journal of Systemic Therapies*, *27*, 5–22.

Index

cancellations 3
case formulation
    you don't have time to carry out full 76
change
    attitude 118
    behaviour 118
    being prepared to accept costs of 17
    change focus if client realises another issue has greater priority 70
    change may happen when person seeks help 7
    combination of attitude/inference/behavioural/environmental 118
    communicate expectations on covertly as well as overtly 32
    environmental 118
    having committed reason to change 17
    if you and client both expect change from SST 31
    inference 118
    inspiring poetry or literature to which client can refer 104
    knowing how to change, and acting on that knowledge 17
    life lessons used in change process 104
    maxims helpful for change process 106
    much can be achieved if client ready to change 25
    recognise it comes in different forms 118
    small change may be sufficient; do not overload them 119
    target for change client's responses to initial reaction 86
    therapeutic change may happen slowly/gradually/quickly/suddenly 26
    what client has done that may have brought about 57
clarity
    check by asking client to share understanding 73
    strive to be clear in all communications with client 72
clients
    additional help if needed 2
    adopt chosen helping stance 64
    allow to determine how much help needed 59
    ask permission to interrupt 71
    ask them to repeat important things they have just said 126
    assess problem using concepts from favoured therapy 81
    attendance not predictable 9

Index

Index